HANDEL

Who Knew What He Liked

M. T. Anderson

illustrated by
Kevin Hawkes

CANDLEWICK PRESS
CAMBRIDGE, MASSACHUSETTS

THIS IS GEORGE FRIDERIC HANDEL.

He looks very satisfied with things. He's smiling a little, as if he's very sure of himself.

You'd have to be sure of yourself to wear a wig that gigantic.

George Frideric Handel

Born in Germany, 1685 — Died in England, 1759

Right from an early age, Handel knew just what he liked. He wanted to study music. His father said he couldn't. His father said nobody ever made any money as a musician. He told the boy to study something that would make him money.

Handel's father was a doctor.

But little Handel knew what he liked. What he liked was music. So he smuggled a clavichord up into the attic without his parents knowing. Late at night, he taught himself to play.

Handel was an unusual boy. Not everyone has the courage to smuggle a clavichord past their parents.

A clavichord is an early version of the piano. As in a piano, the strings of a clavichord are hit with small hammers. Handel also played the harpsichord, *in which the strings are plucked with quills instead, like a big mechanical harp.*

Handel's older brother worked as a servant in a distant castle that belonged to a grand duke. One day, when Handel was about seven, his father decided to go to the castle to visit. Handel wanted to go, too, but his father wouldn't let him. He said little Handel would just get in the way. Handel's father got into his coach and rode off.

He had gone several miles when he looked out the window.

There was Handel, running along behind the coach. Handel said he really wanted to go. He wouldn't let anything stop him.

So his father sighed and let him get in. They traveled together to the duke's castle. They stayed there for some time with Handel's brother.

One day, the duke heard the organ playing in the chapel. He couldn't see anyone at the keyboard. The music was beautiful, full of energy and grace.

The duke asked his servant, "Who is that playing the organ so splendidly?"

The servant said, "My little brother, young Handel."

The duke decided that Handel should be trained as a musician. On hearing this suggestion, Handel's father was angry and said he would not allow it. But the duke convinced him to compromise and let the boy study music and law.

In Handel's day, organists had an assistant to pump a bellows to make the organ play. The bellows were boxes and bags of air that, when squeezed, pedaled, or stretched, blew air through the pipes.

Handel studied first in his own city of Halle, and later, when he was eighteen, in the city of Hamburg. One of his best friends in Hamburg was a composer named Mattheson. They both loved music. In particular, they loved operas. Sometimes they even performed operas together.

Mattheson couldn't get enough opera— especially his own. He would write an opera, and then he would star in it himself. He would often arrange to play a character who died partway through the opera. That way he could jog down and lead the orchestra from the harpsichord. Handel, who'd be playing when Mattheson got there, would have to stop and move aside for his friend.

Handel thought Mattheson was a bit of a pain. One night when Mattheson had killed himself onstage and come down to play the harpsichord, Handel refused to get up. Mattheson threatened him. Handel was very stubborn; he kept right on playing. So right there and then, Mattheson challenged Handel to a duel.

An opera is like a play where everything is sung instead of said.

In Handel's time, orchestras were usually led by the person playing the harpsichord, instead of by a conductor with a baton.

They walked out of the theater into the cold winter's night. They drew their swords and set upon each other in the square. Mattheson thrust his rapier right toward Handel's heart— but luckily the blade hit Handel's coat button, and broke.

Later that night, they went out for a big dinner. After all, they were still good friends. Big dinners always made Handel feel a lot better.

In 1706, Handel went to Italy to travel around and study music and meet the greatest musicians of his day. As always, he made quite an impression with his quick fingers.

He went to the dark and shuttered city of Florence, where he stayed with the wealthy Medici family.

He traveled to Venice, city of canals and palaces, and he lived in the domed and gracious city of Rome, where at concerts and parties and vast church services he met some of the finest musicians of his age. He decided he loved Italian opera more than anything else.

He wrote little dramas and operas for his friends, and staged them in theaters and noble houses. In Rome, where no opera was allowed because it was thought to be sinful, he also set religious texts to music.

He attended parties at palaces, and, wearing magnificent wigs, he ate and he listened and he played to his heart's content. Once he ordered forty-five pounds of snow from the mountains to chill his wine.

In 1711, after a few years in Italy, Handel decided to travel to England. He played music for the queen of England, who told him he was wonderful. Handel was encouraged.

In two weeks, he wrote an opera, and arranged for it to be put on in London. It was called *Rinaldo*, and everybody loved it. One of the special effects was a flock of live birds released in the theater so they'd fly around the audience.

Handel decided that he wanted to stay in England and produce Italian operas there. His father had said he would never make any money writing and playing music. He decided he'd prove his father wrong.

There was only one problem. In general, the English didn't really like opera. They thought it had too much music in it. They didn't understand why people should sing everything.

But Handel knew what he liked, and he was determined to make everyone else see things his way. He decided to dazzle them. He would put on a show that nobody could refuse.

Even though the operas were in Italian, the English audience could follow along with the printed words in the libretto, which is Italian for "little book."

Handel's operas were big and expensive. The stories were about kings and princes and princesses living in far-off, exotic palaces and temples. The scenery would be painted with marvelous columns and glittering jewels. The costumes would be strange and ornate, with plumes, capes, and gems. The characters would sing arias in Italian, some of the most beautiful music ever heard onstage. Then they would stab each other.

And it worked. People started coming to the opera. They were all very impressed with Handel. Since the king and queen of England thought his music was wonderful, all the noblemen and noblewomen went to see him play, and clapped to please the king and queen. Handel's operas were all the rage. Handel would prove his father was wrong.

An aria is what a song in an opera is called.

Though much of Handel's energy went into creating and performing operas, he did other things as well. He taught music to the royal family. He composed pieces for orchestra and pieces for harpsichord; he wrote music for church choirs and music for organ.

For King George I, he wrote his famous *Water Music*. The king wished to travel down the River Thames in a royal barge, with music drifting out over the water. Handel and a whole orchestra drifted along beside him in another boat.

It didn't rain. Nothing sprang a leak. The king loved the music so much he asked for it to be played three times. It must have been a beautiful sight, the barges drifting on that glittering river as the sun set on the warm summer's evening over the domes and spires of antique London.

These entertainments, however, did not always go so well. Several years later, there was a complete disaster.

England and Germany had been at war—the War of the Austrian Succession. In 1749, after the peace treaty was signed and the war declared over, the king of England decided to hold a celebration.

He arranged for an evening of fireworks like few had ever seen before. The king of Germany and he would watch together. He ordered that a special palace be built just for the fireworks. He hired Handel to write music for lots of drums and trumpets so it would sound like battle and bombs. One of the first sections of the fireworks music was supposed to represent the war. Then another was supposed to represent the peace, gentle and ebbing. The last section was supposed to represent everyone's rejoicing.

Instead what happened was the fireworks palace caught on fire and exploded.

People ran. People yelled for water. One side of the palace burned, wildly spitting out rockets and pinwheels. Sparks and embers sailed through the air. The man who'd designed the palace pulled out his sword and attacked the Comptroller of the Fireworks.

No one knows what Handel was doing during all this. Perhaps ducking suavely to save his wig from bright hungry sparks. He didn't let things bother him much.

Not usually, at least.

But things started to get very difficult for him. Some people hated his operas. Someone even published a cartoon making fun of him. It showed him playing the organ surrounded by food, a pig in a wig.

To draw crowds to his operas, Handel hired some of the most famous singers in the world. This immediately caused problems.

Famous singers can be very jealous. Handel's singers complained if he wrote more arias for one of them than the others. They tried to outsing each other. They would stop in the middle of an aria and hold up the whole opera just to skip around from note to note for a while until everyone admitted that they were better than the others. During the performance of a friend's opera, two of Handel's most famous sopranos, Cuzzoni and Faustina, had a disagreement and started slugging each other right onstage. They had to be pulled apart. And people loved it.

But Handel wouldn't let this go too far. He controlled these fiery singers with an iron will.

Once one of his tenors threatened to dive off the stage right into Handel's harpsichord. Handel called his bluff and said that was just fine with him.

He said, "More people will come to see you jump than to hear you sing."

And difficult singers weren't Handel's only problem. A rival opera company started up. The king's son went there in the evenings. Everyone followed him. Soon, Handel's opera house was empty.

Things got worse. John Gay, who once had been a friend of Handel, wrote a musical play called *The Beggar's Opera*. It made fun of Italian operas, and Handel's in particular. Instead of being set in a distant, exotic country, *The Beggar's Opera* was set in London and was in English. It wasn't about kings and queens; it was about cockney merchants and thieves. And instead of using arias, it used popular songs of the day. It made Handel's operas seem overblown and silly.

It had a few songs by Handel in it, because they were so popular. But Handel wasn't very flattered. They were right next to songs called "Cold and Raw," "The Irish Howl," and "Lumps of Pudding."

Handel probably thought the play was funny the first couple of times he saw it. But it was not a joke that grew on him. People were laughing at him.

Here we see Handel lost in despair. He doesn't even have his magnificent wig on.

Handel had spent almost thirty years trying to bring opera to the English. And he felt that he had failed. Comical musical plays like *The Beggar's Opera* were selling out, but no one was coming to Handel's operas anymore.

His opera company ran out of money. It shut down.

Handel grew sick.

He was out of money.

He was out of luck.

He wanted to go home.

He, who had always known what he liked, was finally giving up.

Handel decided to return to Germany. There was nothing else to do.

First, though, he had one last concert series to give, in Dublin, Ireland. The money from the concerts would go to various Irish orphanages. Handel had to write some music for the event.

So Handel set about composing a new piece.

It was called *Messiah*.

Handel thought it would be the last piece he would write in Britain.

The words for the *Messiah* were taken from the Bible. It was an oratorio, or sacred story in music. The words concerned ancient prophecies about the coming of a great king; they suggested these prophecies were fulfilled in the Birth and the Crucifixion of Christ.

Handel wrote the music very quickly, as if possessed. There are many stories about the composition of the *Messiah*: Servants would bring Handel food on a tray; a few hours later, they would return to remove the tray and the food would be untouched. Some say the score was blotched and spattered with Handel's tears.

He put everything into this final piece.

An oratorio is different from an opera in two ways: It isn't acted out, with scenery and costumes, like an opera, and its story is usually taken from the Bible. The word oratorio comes from the Latin word that means "to pray."

And the performances were wonderful. Nobles came from all around and gave Handel money for the concerts and orphanages. People raved about the singers. Many people said they had never heard anything like it before. Some of the arias flowed easily, like cool water in a brook; others scalded, like fire, or cut, like whips. The choruses were noble, like a crowd shouting together for a king who entered in victory.

The *Messiah* was a huge success.

Handel thought maybe he wouldn't go back home to Germany after all.

He had a new plan. He wouldn't give up. He knew what he liked, and one way or another, he would convince everyone else.

He'd go right back to London. He'd forget about those feisty Italian opera stars. They weren't worth it. He'd hire English singers. Instead of staging operas in Italian, he'd write English oratorios. Instead of having huge pieces of scenery showing strange temples and live flocks of birds and fountains of fire, he would just describe those things in his music. He'd make people see them through music alone. And this is what he did.

As the years passed, Handel's oratorios became more and more famous. People played them to celebrate his birthday. They played them to get money for charities and causes.

And they played them to remember him when, in 1759, he died.

After his death, his fame kept spreading. The choirs that sang his music got larger and larger, louder and louder.

As time went on, people sang the *Messiah* in England, in Handel's native Germany, and in the new country called the United States of America. The choirs kept getting bigger. Once the *Messiah* was played by an orchestra of five hundred, with a choir of four thousand people chanting and shouting the music that Handel had once cried over alone in his room.

There are four basic ranges of voice. From the lowest to the highest, they are bass, tenor, alto, and soprano.

Every year, in cities and towns across the world, the *Messiah* is still performed for Christmas and Easter. The most famous part is the "Hallelujah Chorus." When this chorus starts, there is a tradition that the whole audience rises to their feet. It is a moving moment. The music thunders and everyone is smiling.

There is a story that we stand because, years ago, when the king first heard this music, he stood up, and everyone else followed. This story is almost certainly not true, but it is a good story nonetheless.

We can imagine what it would be like if it were true. We can imagine Handel smiling to himself, playing his music. Waggling his wig. Feeling the theater vibrating with his vision, and knowing he's made his point.

Knowing that, in spite of everything, he could do what he liked.

Chronology of Handel's Life

1685	George Frideric Handel is born in Halle, Germany.
1704	Handel fights duel with Mattheson in Hamburg, Germany.
1706	He travels to Italy, where he stays for several years.
1710	Handel travels to England for the first time.
1711	*Rinaldo*, Handel's first London opera, opens.
1717	Handel's *Water Music* is played for King George I.
1727	Handel is naturalized as an English citizen; his Coronation Anthems are performed for the crowning of King George II.
1737	Handel first falls sick with a paralytic disorder that will recur several times.
1741	He writes the *Messiah*.
1742	First performance of *Messiah*, Dublin, Ireland.
1743	First London performance of *Messiah*.
1749	Handel's *Music for the Royal Fireworks* performed to celebrate the Peace of Aix-la-Chapelle.
1751	Handel starts to lose his vision; he will, over the next few years, excuse himself from performances on account of his growing blindness.
1759	Handel dies. His burial in Westminster Abbey is attended by 3,000 people.

Discography

Handel, George Frideric. *Arias for Cuzzoni, Durastanti, Senesino, Montagnana.* Philharmonia Baroque Orchestra. Harmonia Mundi 2907171.

Handel, George Frideric. *Ariodante.* Freiburg Baroque Orchestra. Harmonia Mundi 907146.

Handel, George Frideric. *Israel in Egypt.* Taverner Consort. Virgin 61350.

Handel, George Frideric. *Messiah.* Boston Baroque. Telarc 80322.

Handel, George Frideric. *Messiah.* Chicago Symphony Orchestra. London Classics 14396.

Handel, George Frideric. *Messiah.* English Concert. Archiv 23630.

Handel, George Frideric. *Rinaldo.* Academy of Ancient Music. Decca 467087.

Handel, George Frideric. *Water Musick.* Philharmonia Baroque Orchestra. Harmonia Mundi 907010.

Handel, George Frideric. *Water Music and Music for the Royal Fireworks.* London Classical Players. Virgin Veritas 45265.

Handel, George Frideric. *Water Music and Music for the Royal Fireworks.* Orpheus Chamber Orchestra. Deutsche Grammophon 35390.

Further Reading

There are many excellent biographies of Handel for adult readers — in fact, he was one of the first composers to be the subject of a book-length biography. The three standard modern biographies are Donald Burrows's *Handel* (Oxford: Oxford University Press, 1995), Christopher Hogwood's *Handel* (London: Thames and Hudson, 1984), and Winton Dean's more compact summary in *The New Grove Handel* (New York: W. W. Norton, 1983). Those who are interested in original sources should look at Otto Deutsch's *Handel: A Documentary Biography* (New York: Da Capo Press, 1974). A very good, somewhat more approachable, introduction to Handel's life can be found in Volume 4 of the series entitled The Great Composers: Their Lives and Times: *Baroque Festival: Antonio Vivaldi (1678–1741) and George Frideric Handel (1685–1759)* (Freeport, NY: Marshall Cavendish, 1987); this book is profusely illustrated and includes, for nonmusicians, a helpful listening guide to the major musical works, as well as an intelligent discussion of the world in which Handel lived.

To all the local choirs and choral societies who keep Handel's music alive — M. T. A.   To Hannah Smith, with much gratitude — K. H.

The publisher wishes to thank Ellen T. Harris,
Professor of Music and Theater Arts
at the Massachusetts Institute of Technology.

Text copyright © 2001 by M. T. Anderson
Illustrations copyright © 2001 by Kevin Hawkes

First edition 2001

Library of Congress Cataloging-in-Publication Data

Anderson, M. Tobin.
Handel, who knew what he liked / M. T. Anderson ; illustrated by Kevin Hawkes. — 1st ed.
p.   cm.
Summary: A man who would later compose some of the world's most
beautiful music is shown as a stubborn little boy with a mind of his own.
ISBN 0-7636-1046-1
[1. Handel, George Frideric, 1685–1759—Juvenile fiction.
2. Handel, George Frideric, 1685–1759—Fiction.
3. Composers—Fiction.] I. Hawkes, Kevin, ill. II. Title.
PZ7.A54395 Han 2001   [Fic]—dc21   00-057210

2 4 6 8 10 9 7 5 3 1

Printed in the United States of America

This book was typeset in Truesdell Bold.
The illustrations were done in acrylic.

Candlewick Press 2067 Massachusetts Avenue Cambridge, Massachusetts 02140 visit us at www.candlewick.com

NON PENSIL...

INTERDICTUS ES